S. D. HORTON

Outlast all of the denials, declines, and delays of life!

I FORGOT TO BE AFRAID

UNVEILING KEY STRATEGIES TO RELEASING YOURSELF FROM THE CHAINS OF FEAR

I FORGOT TO BE AFRAID

S.D. Horton Enterprises
P.O. Box 1612
Alamogordo, NM 88311

Copyright © 2012 by S.D. Horton
Printed in the United States of America

ISBN: 978-0615636252
Library of Congress Control Number: 2012909350
Publishing by: SD Horton Enterprises

Editorial assistance by: Delgar Publishing

Cover design by: Brian C. Harris

Scripture references are quoted from various translations of the Holy Bible.

All rights reserved. No portion of this book may be used without the written permission of the publisher, with the exception of brief excerpts in magazine articles, reviews, etc.

Table of Contents

Acknowledgment   v

Special Thanks   vi

Introduction   vii

CHAPTER 1
Who Told You to Be Afraid?... 1

CHAPTER 2
It's Not That Big a Deal!..13

CHAPTER 3
What About the Economy?.. 25

CHAPTER 4
It's Time For a Name Change...................................... 35

CHAPTER 5
Kick the Habit.. 47

CHAPTER 6
Developing Amnesia... 55

CHAPTER 7
No More Excuses!... 63

Faith Strategies   73

About the Author   85

✦ Acknowledgment ✦

To my lovely wife, Cheryl, who continues to provide the much needed support that enables me to chase my dreams! Thanks for always being there for me.

To three of the most precious children a parent could ever be blessed to have, DeAundre, Jasmine, and Jalen. I wish to thank you for being loving and obedient children. You are my legacy!

In loving memory of my late father, George Horton. Your inspiration continues to push me forward. All my achievements clearly demonstrate that your impact still lives on. I miss you dad! Your legacy continues through your sons!

To my mother, Winfred Horton, who has always encouraged me to be the best I can be. Thanks for raising such a wonderful son!

To my spiritual father, mentor, and senior pastor, Dr. Mikel Brown, and First Lady Debra Brown, for your undying love and unfailing support. I am blessed to be one of your many sons. I am able to celebrate being an author mainly because of your example of authorship. Thank you so much for being that timely spark of inspiration and encouragement to come into my life when you did!

✦ Special Thanks ✦

Special thanks to all of the men and women of God who continue to show their support for me!

Dr Mikel and First Lady Debra Brown
Dr Bill and Pastor Sharon Roberts
Pastor Charles and First Lady Talisha Bennett
Bishop Jimmy and First Lady Linda Copeland
Pastor Frank and First Lady Portia Holmes
Pastor Dana Brazell
Pastor Arlena Harris-Gilreath

Introduction

Medical doctors, scientists, and memory experts have long since established the fact that our long-term memories have the ability to capture and store all the sensory information acquired from the moment we are born to the time we die. If true, the implications are astounding. What this suggests is that we literally have the potential to recall every one of our moments of triumphs, as well as each instance of defeat ever experienced.

But we must be careful to recognize that our human nature teaches us to focus more on the negative experiences than on the positive ones. Thus, we are more prone to replay over and over our defeats rather than reliving our triumphs.

In his letter to the Christians in Rome, the Apostle Paul encouraged the saints to be transformed by the renewing of their minds so that God's perfect will would be proven. If we too would follow this instruction, we could train our minds to focus more on the positive aspects of life rather than getting mired in all the negative debris that life will no doubt present. When we focus our thoughts and efforts on our triumphs, we will soon develop the instinctive habit of repeating them time and again. In doing so, our lives are constantly being transformed, our minds are being renewed, and our faith is dramatically increasing. The end result will be a long-term memory full of more triumphs than defeats! And when faced with moments of crisis, you will discover that your reservoir is filled with all the faith-building material needed to make your dreams a reality...simply because you forgot to be afraid!!!

CHAPTER 1

WHO TOLD YOU TO BE AFRAID?

1

WHO TOLD YOU TO BE AFRAID?

In its most generic sense, fear is defined as distress or anxiety one feels regarding impending danger, discomfort, or pain. Although we are all born with a certain level of fear that is the result of man's fallen, sin nature, it seems to only grow and worsen as we get older and surround ourselves with others of like precious doubt. Yes, you read that right! We have a tendency to hang around other individuals who have never learned how to shake this epidemic contagion themselves. As a result, we begin to reciprocate the process by transmitting our phobias to those with whom we come in contact.

In essence, fear is a learned response that then manifests in wide range of counterproductive or destructive behaviors. As that old saying goes, "monkey see, monkey do!" Unless taught otherwise, children will undoubtedly be infected with the plague of fear that gets imposed upon them by their immediate surroundings. The longer they live in certain fear-inducing environments, the more their actions will mimic certain uncontrollable involuntary muscle reflex responses to certain stimuli—always reacting, never able to be proactive.

Fear is no respecter of persons. It torments all without regard to race, gender, age, or socio-economic status. It could care less about your academic credentials, financial status, or how well you may articulate. Fear simply needs a willing vessel to carry out its objectives.

Naked and Afraid

Adam is a great example of someone who became a willing vessel for fear's end-game strategy to render one useless. Here we have an individual who was the prototype of God's desired intention for mankind. Adam was handed authority and dominion over all that God created, and yet he forfeited it because he was too afraid to say no to his wife! And once you submit to fear, it will expose you for the coward you are and then depose you from your throne of your birthright! That is why God asked Adam the very familiar question, "Who told you that you were naked?" In other words, who told you how to operate in fear? Fear alone caused Adam to hide when he when he become aware of his nakedness.

And once you submit to fear, it will expose you for the coward you are.

Likewise, it is fear that causes us to hide the things we do not want anyone else to see. For that reason, you must expose your negatives to the light where they can be destroyed, in order that you may receive the peace you deserve. The longer they are hidden, the more time you waste in needless suffering.

God equipped Adam with dominance, but He also empowered Adam with the right to choose. Consequences, whether good or bad, will always follow the choices you make. Every road leads to a final destination. Whichever road you choose is up to you. Therefore, as God once suggested, please choose the road that leads to life, so that you and your descendants could live a blessed life!

The Fail-Proof Plan

What Adam failed to understand was that God had already set him up with a fail-proof plan to succeed. Just as Dorothy was required to follow the yellow brick road to get to her destination, all Adam had to do was to follow the plan of God in order to maintain his dominion over all God's creation. Instead, he chose option B. And ever since Adam's calamitous decision, all of humanity has been on a downward spiral. Thank God for Jesus, who is a repairer of the breach!!

When the Word became flesh and entered the earth in the form of Jesus (considered the last Adam), He had one thing in mind...to restore dominion back to man. But there is a catch! Anyone who wishes to experience this dominion must first agree to abide by all the terms and conditions of His last-edition, fail-proof plan.

If you set out trying to operate according to the dictates of fear and emotions, you will soon discover that you disqualify yourself from the plan's benefits. This excellent plan demands your attention and obedience! As Jesus told Nicodemus one dark night, you must be born-again to operate in this type of spiritual dominion! Option B did not work in the Garden of Eden, and it sure won't work today!

A Clearly Defined Picture

Abstract art is defined as art that may or may not bear a resemblance to its subject. While it may be a much appreciated form of artistic expression to art lovers, abstract art fails to clearly capture and define the true purpose and meaning of the object itself.

On the contrary, God's word and His way of doing things are clearly revealed in both written expression and prophetic utterances. But what do you have when something is left to interpretation? Chaos!!! My mentor once said that when a picture

I FORGOT TO BE AFRAID

is not clearly defined, people define it for themselves. Anytime a standard is not publicized and declared, people are left to form their own opinions, leaving chaos to ensue.

Faith is birthed in unity, while fear is birthed out of chaos. That is why it is very important for us to stick with the standard! You will never fail when doing so! It amazes me that we could ever think we have things all figured out. Oftentimes we fall into the trap of thinking that just because events are not happening according to our timetable, then something must be wrong with what we are doing. That is a far cry from the truth! Anytime you operate by faith, the process will never happen according to your time estimates. It may be long in some cases, and short in others. Nonetheless, patience is needed.

Faith is birthed in unity, while fear is birthed out of chaos.

Do not give up just because you do not "see" the desired result(s) right away. Stop allowing fear to suggest to you that quitting is an option! If you hold on, you will see the defined picture more clearly.

Educate and Eradicate

To experience consistent success, you must do an inventory of your life. Consistent success demands consistent faith. Therefore, you cannot afford to have anybody or anything in your inner circle of influence with the potential hinder your progress. There are too many people in this world who simply do not know how to walk in faith. Do not continue to be one of them. As my mentor once said, "having faith does not mean you are not challenged by doubts. Doubts are present because you do have faith. The thing about faith is that if you don't have it, you can't understand it and how it works. And, if you do, no explanation is necessary."

There are too many people in this world who simply do not know how to walk by faith.

For that reason alone, you need to conduct a complete life inventory and self-examination. You must keep the people and things which enhance your life, and rid yourself of those which are detrimental to your future. How much you believe in yourself and how far you wish to journey in life

I FORGOT TO BE AFRAID

will determine whether or not someone else is considering putting YOU in their deleted associates file or choosing to keep you around. But for the moment, you must decide who qualifies to stay and who simply must be cut off!

Remember, surrounding yourself with faithful people will definitely be a benefit to you and your future. Negative people, however, demand too much of your valuable time and attention. Negativity always makes you tired. There is an old adage that says, "There is no rest for the weary." What a powerful and true statement!

Faith, however, causes you to enter into a restful state of mind. There is no need to worry when you operate in God's assurance. When you understand that God is your ultimate provider, you will never be in want; you will lay down in green pastures; you will be led beside the still and restful waters; your soul will be refreshed and restored; you will be led in the paths of righteousness; and though you walk through the shadow of death, you will have no fear of evil!

There is no need to worry when you operate in God's assurance.

I don't know about you, but I think that entering into the eradication process is worth it since I will experience this type of life! Your prayer from this point forward must be, "God, surround me with people who love, honor, and respect You! Send people into my life who choose to do things Your way!"

PSALM 27:1
(Amplified Bible)

The LORD is my Light and my Salvation - whom shall I fear or dread? The Lord is the Refuge and Stonghold of my life - of whom shall I be afraid?

Who Told You To Be Afraid?

CHAPTER 2

IT'S NOT THAT BIG A DEAL!

2

IT'S NOT THAT BIG A DEAL!

Have you ever asked yourself, "Now why did I just do that?" If you have ever done an honest assessment of your past, you would likely conclude that you have in fact experienced situations where you simply wasted too much time on things that really did not matter, only to realize that it was too late to reverse tracks because you had already crossed the proverbial Rubicon, or point of no return. And although you may have gained a ton of experience while stumbling through those situations, you are left to lament the fact that precious time wasted on inconsequential indulgences can never be recovered.

As I was driving through Manchester, Georgia one day, I began to think about life and how much time is wasted on things that are insignificant. We have a tendency to allow temporary situations and setbacks to become bigger than they truly are. Consequently, out of naivety, we end up birthing permanent adverse consequences while in the midst of very temporary circumstances. Repeating this unwise behavior, my friend, will set you back tremendously! We must learn to distinguish between those situations with long-term implications versus those transient episodes that are of short duration and little significance.

You would be amazed how much time you waste by allowing certain people to influence your decisions in life. For example, allowing naysayers and negative people to remain in your inner circle is a big waste of time. While you are concerned about hurting their feelings instead of letting them go, you are undoubtedly squandering precious time as result of your indecision. You must detach yourself from the fear of being alone! Being "alone" is not always a bad position. While I am a huge advocate of being around positive people, I also understand that there are times when you need to separate yourself from people...especially negative people...and allow yourself to dream. Dreams can become reality when you detach yourself from negative influences.

Being "alone" is not always a bad position.

If you ever want to find a multitude of examples of people who waste precious time making a big deal out of minor things, you need look no further than the popular social media venues of our day. A very brief examination of Facebook, Twitter, and Myspace dialogue will confirm my contention. Based on the majority of most people's post updates on these sites, you can determine a person's fears, challenges, and regrets. Most readers can even determine whether or not a person is on course to go far in life.

It is little wonder why many companies have resorted to tracking the social media activities of their employees. They have found that they are able to glean more freely-offered information from these sites than they are legally able to require employees to divulge. I am constantly amazed by the intimate comments people post for public consumption. Businesses owners now realize how easy it is to gain access into the minds of their employees in order to find out certain information that was once beyond their reach...such as how their employees deal with stress and react under pressure.

I can imagine many employers asking, "Would they make a big deal about an insignificant situation, or will they learn to overcome?" Nowadays, many employees are indeed losing their jobs because of what their employers are discovering about them in cyberspace. The prevailing view is that what you discuss on social networking sites becomes public domain information...and consequently actionable by one's employers.

This is one of the many reasons why we should not fall into the trap of turning mountains into mole hills. Some things are simply not worth the time! Precious time is being wasted, and time is

It's Not That Big a Deal!

definitely not on the procrastinator's side! You must find out what is causing you to be distracted. What have you allowed to become a mountain when it was first presented as a mole hill?

Some things are simply not worth the time!

it's Just a Bark!

At the time of this writing, my youngest son has a fear of certain animals, especially dogs. Needless to say, his constant display of fear irks me to no end! My question to him is, "Son, who taught you to fear dogs?" Maybe it was a movie he saw on television. Or maybe a pretend buddy told him how scary dogs are because of their loud, intimidating barking. In either case, those are not legitimate reasons to be afraid of dogs. Whether it is a small puppy, or a large Rottweiler, my son will run and scream until the very sight of the dog is removed from his view. So what causes grown, mature adults to act like my son when it comes to certain disconcerting situations in life?

Let us take a trip down memory lane. If you can recall, dogs tend to respond to us based upon our actions. For example, if you ran at the sound of its bark, the dog in turn began to chase you. What we did not realize as children is that all animals are designed by God to be subject to man's authority. But Adam's fall from grace changed all that for us. Today, we are subject to the very things over which we once had unmistakable dominion. Back in the garden, Adam forfeited man's authority on the planet, and we have been operating in fear ever since, instead of faith.

Beloved, the bark was only a loud noise that was designed to cloud our view of the truth. It was a diabolical plan that only worked because we surrendered our authority to something that was designed to be subject to us!

My heart really goes out to individuals (mostly wives) who have endured any type of spousal abuse in their marriages. Whether it is physical, emotional, verbal, or sexual, all types of abuses are detrimental to the psyche of an individual. That is why I admire those who have exercised the courage to eventually walk away from an abusive relationship. They are individuals who simply refused to allow the bark to become a bite!

It's Not That Big a Deal!

Again, the bark is designed to cloud your view of the truth. Once you give the bark more power than it deserves, it will begin to affect everything else in your life. I have heard too many stories of daughters and sons being molested by their fathers because the mothers did not know how to confront the cowardly abuser. In some cases, the mother was also being abused. The bark turned into a bite and began to affect everyone who was directly and indirectly involved. That is why it is imperative to deal with the situation in its infancy. Stand up to that dog and let him know that you will not tolerate his barking any longer!

...the bark is designed to cloud your view of the truth.

As adults, we may no longer carry around a childish fear of dogs, but there yet remain other things to which we have relinquished our authority. The barks from life's varied skirmishes have caused us to make drastic and sometimes unnecessary changes in our lives. As stated earlier, we have made the fatal mistake of making bad decisions that carry long-term negative consequences in the midst of temporary circumstances. If we continue to allow this diabolical plan to run its course, we will never begin to realize the great potential that lies within us!

I Choose to Smile

As you should have noticed by now, life has a tendency to throw curve balls at us on a constant basis. I have come to realize that it is not the curve ball itself that is the issue; it is my reaction to what is being pitched to me. My reaction to the pitch will determine whether I hit a homerun, or just simply strike out. Some of us have chosen to strike out too many times! We unwisely decide to hang our heads low when intense circumstances become seemingly unbearable. Tears of joy become tears of frustration because we fail to learn how to hit the ball! There is a famous quote that says, "When life gives you lemons, make lemonade!" In other words, your reaction will determine your outcome. Stop selling yourself short! You are much better than you think you are!

It's Not That Big a Deal!

When life gets tough, you must choose to smile! I choose to smile because I have learned how to hit the curve balls that come my way. How??? By simply learning who is pitching, and why this type of pitch is coming to me. For example, when bills flood my mailbox, I do not place the blame on the devil! If I created the bills, I own up to them!

When life gets tough, you must choose to smile!

At the same time, I have determined in my mind that God's work is not going to suffer because of the bills I created. No money gets diverted from God's house to the pockets of my creditors. I continue to honor God with my tithes AND offerings. Then I act upon the fact that God has given me the ability to create wealth (Deuteronomy 8:18). And with that ability, I create the wealth to pay off my debts, so that I can be more of a blessing to God's work. Homerun!

The curve of the pitch is designed to cause you to walk in fear. You were, however, designed by God to walk by faith and not by sight. But you must make the conscience decision to do either. My mentor once encouraged me to be a creator of circumstances, and not a creature of them. With that said, I made the conscience decision that I will create faith-filled circumstances in my life from now on! I choose to no longer listen to the bark or pay any undue attention to the curve balls thrown in my direction. Those are only distractions designed by the enemy to cause me to lay aside my confidence. I refuse to waste time on the temporary (fear), when it is the eternal (faith) that is going to sustain me.

You must get to the point where you are tired of striking out.

You must get to the point where you are tired of striking out. In the game of baseball, great hitters have learned how to consistently hit the pitches of great pitchers. Since he has been playing professional baseball, Albert Pujos has arguably been the most consistent homerun hitter in Major League Baseball. How did he become so successful where many other hitters have failed? Albert has a knack of studying his opponents' weaknesses and capitalizing on them. His example has broad implications.

Too much focus is being placed on how the

It's Not That Big a Deal!

devil is wrecking havoc in our homes and in our finances; but not enough focus is being placed on us getting to know our enemy's ways so that we can wreck havoc on his kingdom! If we know that his ultimate objective is to steal, kill, and destroy, why don't we become the aggressor and disarm his camp before he has the chance to get to ours?

We must learn to become homerun hitters in life! No matter what type of pitch is thrown at you, know that you have the potential to succeed at hitting each and every one of them!!! But potential that is not used is simply power that slowly fades. The less you use something, the more difficult it becomes to call upon later. Therefore, we must exercise our muscles more consistently. As you habitually swing at those pitches, you begin to develop levels of tenacity that will be hard to ignore. Soon, the pitcher will begin to realize that no matter what pitch is thrown your way, he knows the end result will be a home run with a smile on your face, as you take your victory lap around the bases!

CHAPTER 3

WHAT ABOUT THE ECONOMY?

3

WHAT ABOUT THE ECONOMY?

As an avid reader of the Bible, I have come to realize that God desires for me to have more than enough when it comes to material wealth. I also realize that great responsibility is attached to my role as a steward. One of the prerequisites to experiencing true success is that I must do things His way!

Many people have been able to amass great fortunes by applying biblical principles, without ever committing to the one true God who established them. The majority of God's natural principles work for mankind irrespective of our spiritual relationship to Him.

But I have chosen to apply those same principles AND have an intimate relationship with the principle-Giver! So, to experience true success, you must have a relationship with God, through Jesus Christ, Who gives you the power/ability to create wealth for covenant purposes (Deuteronomy 8:18)!

Jesus once said that there will always be the poor among you. Now, based on other supporting scriptures, Jesus was not suggesting that certain people are born destined to a life of poverty. What He was saying is...again based on other supporting scriptures...that people are simply going to refuse to apply the basic principles in order to attain a better earthly lifestyle.

I, however, am not one of those individuals! I choose conduct my affairs God's way. I understand fully that simply living a Godly life will bring about a certain measure of persecution. And wanting more than enough, as the Bible declares (Mark 10:30), will no doubt illicit outrage on behalf of naysayers. With that said, I would rather have more than enough together with the persecution so that I can advance God's kingdom rather than settling for poverty, and dying a slow, uneventful death. I would rather do it God's way!

A Nation Under God?

It is a well known fact that our great nation is experiencing tremendous economic hardship. The political parties are pointing the finger at each other as the cause for our failing economy. The Republican Party is blaming the Democratic Party. The Democratic Party is blaming the Republican Party, The Tea Party, and everyone else! Citizens are blaming either the previously-elected Republican President, or the current Democratic President. No one wants to take the blame.

What is truly devastating is that born-again believers affiliated with either, or even neither of these political parties, are pointing fingers instead of weighing-in with solutions! We are the ones with real answers, yet we refuse to provide the way of escape. In truth, the born-again believer should not be negatively affected by our nation's failing

I FORGOT TO BE AFRAID

economy; for we have dual citizenship. Our heavenly nation tells us (citizens) that we are the head, and not the tail! Our Commander-in-Chief informs His people that all things are possible to him that believes! So why are we pointing fingers? Better yet, why do we vote for the candidate who wants you to suffer financially while he/she lives lavishly?

> *Our heavenly nation tells us that we are the head, and not the tail!*

So who or what is the culprit? Who is causing you to point the finger? What is causing you to vote the way you vote? Why don't you believe that you can do all things through Christ? The answer is: FEAR!

Many media outlets ensure that fear is the reason why you react the way you do. It has been working for decades now! As the saying goes, "if it ain't broke, don't try to fix it!" They want you to operate out of fear as opposed to faith. They will make a big stink about how bad the economy is so that you spend ample time worrying and depending on bail-out plans to succeed. A few of our government subsidized programs are good,

What About the Economy?

but only for a season. Imagine how beneficial our Welfare program would be if only it were used to be a temporary stop-gap measure instead of a permanent fixture in our society! Whether we want to see it or not, our nation is being trained to be dependent on the government, rather than the principles of God.

Born-again believers, however, should know better. We should see that this is definitely a diabolical plan of Satan himself! Again, God has created us to walk by faith. In other words, He is to be our ONLY source for all things. How can we say we love God when we do not trust Him at His word? He has a proven track record!

God's economy will never fail!

God's economy will never fail! He will never resort to panic mode because His ways are eternal and secure. Likewise, we should not resort to panic mode because all of God's promises are yea and amen! Success is always the result of doing things God's way. He has a fail-proof plan that no man can derail.

Don't Interrupt the Cycle

Throughout my years of counseling individuals and couples, I have discovered that people simply do not want to manage their finances God's way! What people have failed to understand is that God's economy will never succumb to recession, regression, or depression. So, why are so many born-again believers afraid of God's process? History reveals to us that people have a tendency to complicate processes instead of keeping them simple. In doing so, they interrupt God's reciprocal laws that govern sowing and reaping.

Anyone who understands farming understands that you cannot have a harvest without first planting a seed. The seed for an apple tree will always be an apple seed. Likewise, the seed to more money will always be money. It is a law that has been established in the earth by God (Genesis 8:22). If you sow love seeds, do not expect a money harvest. The seed always produces after its own kind.

You cannot be fearful of giving. You must sow your seed in order to experience a harvest. You cannot expect a harvest if you have not sown your seed. The number of people who expect otherwise is astronomically high!   Dr. Mikel Brown once said that it is considered insanity to expect different results by doing the same mediocre things. Do not be afraid to change the way you handle your finances. If doing one thing results in little to no harvest, it is time to change your game plan.

You cannot be fearful of giving.

Satan has a diabolical plan in the economic arena, as well. He understands that if the cycle of giving and reaping can be interrupted, God's kingdom cannot advance, God's people will not prosper, and his evil kingdom will continue to spread. Therefore, God's people must take a stand! We can no longer afford to be in the background. We must overcome the fear of change so that we can experience the positive effects of God's economy!

Source vs. Resource

Whenever you confuse the relationship between a source and a resource, you become a person most miserable! A popular, yet frequently misquoted scripture in the bible says that the love of money is the root of all evil. Many people will often leave out the "the love of" portion of the scripture for various reasons. One of the main reasons is that there is a gross misunderstanding of the distinction between a source and a resource. As a matter of fact, money is so misunderstood that Jesus said that we cannot serve both it (money) and God.

Money must always be regarded as simply the resource it is! It is only a tool used to enable us to achieve certain ends in life. Once you grasp this reality, you will develop a healthy appreciation for the money over which you merely exercise certain stewardship responsibilities. Having this perspective, you will never confuse the resource of money with God who forever remains the source.

God never intended for us to place so much attention on the resource. He wants us to concentrate on Him as the Source. When we seek Him and His way of doing things, everything else, including money, will be given to us. Remember, Jesus wants the economy of His church to thrive! And since His church is on earth, money is the tool that is used to advance His kingdom. The Source is

What About the Economy?

never absent of His resources. Therefore God will continue to ensure that His kingdom will ALWAYS have the necessary funds to flourish. There is already a system in place for that (tithes and offerings).

The Source is never absent of His resources.

Again, the money is only a tool! Around the world, it is used to take care of church matters, as well as illegal drug transactions. It is also used to pay bills, buy houses, purchase vehicles, pay allowances, invest in IRAs, buy lottery tickets, and to bail alleged criminals out of jail. Jesus even used it to pay His and Peter's taxes. Money has no intrinsic value. It is neither good nor evil. It is blind and has no regard for race, color, creed, age, or gender. Yet it is one of the most powerful tools on earth! How you use it determines whether you view it as a source or a resource.

CHAPTER 4

IT'S TIME FOR A NAME CHANGE

4

IT'S TIME FOR A NAME CHANGE

Believe it or not, there was a time when naming a child was an important occasion. It used to be that the names parents would assign to their children would be based on something of significance, such as the name of an important historical figure, a key event in history, or something related to the child's destiny in life.

In Jewish culture, children are named after a relative or are given a name that corresponds with a word with significant meaning. For example, the biblical name Abraham means "father of many nations". There are famous people who have decided to change their names to honor others who may have had a positive influence in their lives. Dr. Martin Luther King, Jr. was born with the first name Michael. It is reported that he and his father changed their names to honor Martin Luther, the German Protestant who renounced Catholicism in order to align his life with the more accurate "faith without works, justification by faith" biblical philosophy.

The aforementioned patriarch, Abraham, experienced a name change based on a change in covenant relationship between him and God. His previous name was Abram, which means "exalted father". Even his grandson Jacob experienced a name change under drastic circumstances, going from Jacob to Israel.

As a kid, I desperately desired to have my first name changed to one with a more masculine overtone, since I did not like the unisex appeal of Stacey. Later, I learned that my first name means "one who is fertile". No wonder I was able to produce three kids in just three at bats!

As with names, mentalities and personality types have a tendency to be passed down from parents to their children. Parents who have experienced poverty all their lives usually pass along that same condition to their children. Fathers who are alcoholics tend to have sons who follow in those same footsteps. Furthermore, mothers who have children out of wedlock oftentimes see a repeat of this same distressing behavioral aspiration with their daughters. I personally know three mothers who also became grandmothers in their early to mid-thirties.

For some not so easily explainable reason, we tend to pass along our bad traits to subsequent generations. My personal theory is that we refuse to develop enough good traits to overshadow or outweigh the bad ones. Once the bad traits take firm root in our lives, it becomes difficult to ignore them.

From Victim to Victor

Many of our past bad decisions caused us to see ourselves in a negative light. These decisions oftentimes even encouraged others to stigmatize us for life. Males and females who have children out of wedlock are commonly referred to as "baby daddies" and "baby mommas", respectively. People who constantly lie are referred to as liars. People who possess low self-esteem are often labeled as victims. So, how can we remove these negative labels from our lives?

People with victim mentalities tend to be emotion-driven, brought on by constantly living in fear of some sort. Because of the nature of our emotions, it is very unwise to go through life basing decisions on our unpredictable feelings. That is why God wants us to react to our circumstances based solely on His word! Even when your emotions lead you to make a good decision, it is still dangerous! Once you develop a habit of depending on them, they will inevitably lure you into a snare from which you will not easily be able to free yourself. But God's word is always reliable!

...God's word is always reliable!

According to God's word, you are never

supposed to define yourself as a victim, especially if you are born again! When you surrendered your life to Christ, you received a new birth certificate. Your first certificate defined you as a victim; but your new one declares that you are a victor!!! If you are not yet born again, it behooves you to switch your allegiance to God and receive your status change. Your new nature will afford you so many better promises than your old nature ever could.

Better Promises

In your old nature, you were destined for failure, lack, sickness, pain, fear, and needless suffering. Even when you experienced a few good seasons, they did not last long because you always returned to your default settings. You were stuck between a rock and a hard place. There was neither light at the end of the tunnel, nor hope at the end of the rainbow. You were doomed to inconsistency because you always made decisions out of fear due to your lack of understanding of how faith works.

But since you pledged your fidelity to the Lord, you are now guaranteed better promises! In your new nature, you are destined to success, good health, love, and faith. You now have direction in life because God's word is your compass. Consistency is now a habit because your default settings are set in alignment with the word of God! Emotionally, you are stable because you walk by faith and not by fear. Your emotions are under control because they are now under the influence of the Holy Spirit. All in all, you now have access to better promises!

You now have direction in life because God's word is your compass.

Reach for the Top

In 2005, my mentor preached a sermon entitled "Reach for the Top". This message still resonates loudly with me, even to this day! In the sermon, he stated that the best fruit is at the top of the tree, so you must be willing to do what is necessary to get the best fruit. People who settle for the already-fallen fruit are those who choose to settle for what is given to them, no matter how spoiled the fruit may be. This is a perfect depiction of someone who operates in fear. Better yet, it depicts someone who fails to understand how to

It's Time For a Name Change

attain the better promises that are available to him or her.

Just because the better promises are available to you does not mean you know how to gain access to them. Unbeknownst to many, faith demands corresponding action! You must do the practical in order to receive the promises. Are you willing to do what is necessary to get what you desire? The scriptures encourage us to fight the good fight of faith! Since it is a good fight, faith is definitely worth fighting for!

...faith demands corresponding action!

All of my closest friends are people who know how to fight! I cannot afford to befriend quitters. You must choose to surround yourself with winners. You are known by the company you keep. If you have friends who are consistently using their faith to reach for the top, you will likely exercise similar tenacity to reach your goals, as well.

For example, my wife has received a promotion every year since 2006. She is an example of a friend who refuses to quit! I myself have received a promotion twice since 2005. I have also received an increase in my income due to book sales, speaking engagements, and various other endeavors. I simply refuse to settle for less than my entitled share of life's precious spoils!

It's My World

If you read the Bible often, you will clearly see that God is very wise. He is also very powerful! He created the world how He wanted it to be. Everything is beautiful in His sight. You could also see that God produced after His own kind.

Therefore, since I am created after His similitude and likeness, I am also a creator of my world! I possess the authority to form it the way I would like it to be. That means that if I desire only positive people in my world, it is my prerogative to have just that! With that, I also realize that I must live with the consequences of what I create. For that reason, it is imperative that my world is aligned with the promises of God. I cannot afford to

I am the creator of my world!

It's Time For a Name Change

deviate from God's way of doing things. Any other way would simply be a monumental waste of time!

Dr. Brown once told me that I cannot complain about the things I choose to tolerate. That is why it is such a privilege to have the ability to command my environment. Just as God commands His environment, I, too command mine. God's word says that he who tells lies will not tarry in His sight. Why? Liars will not stand before Him simply because they are a direct contradiction to His nature. Therefore, if God does not allow certain people to continue in His presence, why should I? I am no longer a victim! I am a victor! I acknowledge and operate in my God-given authority. And since it is my world, I have decided to do things God's way!

I am no longer a victim. I am a victor!

Never apologize to anyone for having high standards! People have the tendency to place you in a box because of how they may see you. They may feel that you do not deserve certain things because of the color of your skin, your height, or even where you are from.

I have a friend who, like me, only prefers to have leather seats in his vehicles. He absolutely refuses to purchase a vehicle that does not come with leather seats. Guess what? It is his world and that is his choice! Likewise, you have preferences that others may not agree with. You may prefer a Lexus over a Ford. Or even a Mercedes over a BMW. It does not make you better than anyone else. It is merely an indication that you know how you like your life structured! So, don't apologize! It is your world!

It's Time For a Name Change

CHAPTER 5

KICK THE HABIT

5

KICK THE HABIT

According to recent research conducted by the Centers for Disease Control and Prevention (CDC), the adverse health effects from smoking cigarettes account for nearly 443,000 deaths per year in the United States. The research also indicates that lung cancer is not the only disease that is acquired from smoking. Smoking also causes coronary heart disease, which is the leading cause of death in the United States. Like the results from smoking, living with the habit of fear has a tendency to spread through your life like a wildfire. And just as thorns can choke the life out of healthy plants, it is the nature of fear to stifle the positive effects of faith. You must make a deliberate decision to kick the unhealthy habit of living by fear!

Extended Life

It is safe to say that those who have kicked the habit of smoking have extended their time here on earth. Imagine how much it would benefit the kingdom of God if you decided to kick the habit of fear by operating in faith! I could safely say that your very life will be extended...and enjoyed...when you refuse to be afraid to operate in faith.

The wonderful thing about faith is that it causes you undertake challenges you would never have imagined possible. According to the word of God, the woman with the issue of blood was not healed because she touched the hem of Jesus' garment. She was healed, as Jesus stated, because of her faith. As a result, the condition of her life was dramatically upgraded, and perhaps even extended.

Likewise, the woman from Canaan desired for her daughter to be healed by Jesus. Even after Jesus denied her request, she refused to allow fear to cripple her faith. Jesus acknowledged her great faith, and her daughter was healed from that moment. As a result of the healing, the daughter's life was no doubt extended. So, are you going to kick the bad habit of living by fear so that your life can also be extended?

Faith Demands a Yes!

When you do not receive what you believe, never point the finger at God as if He is holding a good thing from you. He promised that He would not withhold any good thing from you, so do not blame Him! Just as Jesus told the woman with the issue of blood, it is according to your faith. We are often stuck in only believing that "with God, all things are possible." That goes without saying! We need to transition into also believing that "all things are possible to him or her that believes." Even the devil has been unjustly blamed for man's failure to believe. The ball is in your court! Will you choose to believe?

I FORGOT TO BE AFRAID

Another wonderful aspect of faith is that it always demands a response of yes! In the examples listed above, the women refused to accept no for an answer. The woman with the issue of blood suffered for 12 years with her affliction. She also suffered loss of income and loss of dignity. But she refused to allow those things to keep her from receiving her yes response! Her faith demanded a yes, even when her body did not agree. Fear may have been present, but faith always trumps fear!

Fear may be present, but faith always trumps fear!

I am sure the Canaanite woman understood what she was getting into before she decided to approach Jesus about her situation. She fully understood that she was not a Jew. Despite the fact that Jesus referred to her as a dog, her faith still cried out desperately for a yes response. She refused to pull the race card. She also refused to allow certain immaterial facts about her social standing to throw her off track and keep her from claiming the objective of her faith, despite the fact

Kick the Habit

that Jesus was under no obligation to grant this non-Jew her request. She was willing to settle for the crumbs of what belonged to someone else. Needless to say, she received her yes response ahead of schedule!

There are plenty of other biblical examples that can be listed in this chapter. But it does no good to list any of them if you do not believe you are able to kick the habit like many of our biblical ancestors chose to do. If you want a better job, keep searching, applying, asking, and believing until you receive your yes. It matters not how many people before received no responses. It does not even matter if you have received several no's yourself! What matters is whether you are still willing to fight the good fight of faith! Is she worth fighting for? Are you willing to outlast all of the denials, declines, and delays until you receive your thumbs up? Beloved, trust me, it will be worth your perseverance of faith to hang in there. Kick fear out of your life and allow your faith to shine!

What matters is whether you are willing to fight the good fight of faith!

The Ride of a Lifetime

I have no experience with drug use, smoking cigarettes, or drinking alcohol, but I have heard that there is a delightful "high" associated with each of them. While the high is only temporary, it appears, for many, to outweigh the many unhealthy side effects. But I am here to tell you that there is no high comparable to the one you receive when you consistently operate by faith. Living by faith is a lifetime journey. It always propels you ahead of the crowd.

People who operate by faith are often viewed as prideful. Their confidence in God is typically misinterpreted as arrogance. Having confidence is different from being prideful. People who place their trust in God understand what they are called to do without the desire to compete or compare themselves with others, while people who are prideful always see themselves as better than others.

Confident people understand that we all possess the potential to be great, while prideful people only see themselves as the great ones. When it comes to operating from the standpoint of confident trust in God, there can be no compromise. There is no time to compete and compare, since we are all in this thing together. This is definitely a lifetime journey, and I plan to thoroughly enjoy the ride!

CHAPTER 6
DEVELOPING AMNESIA

6

DEVELOPING AMNESIA

No matter who I talk to, the overall consensus is that it is easier to remember our negative life experiences more than the positive ones. The primary reason is that the pain of trauma, setback, or disappointment is not an emotion easily lost to time. The memories associated with pain command more attention and linger at the forefront of our hearts and minds longer than the joys of life. I am sure this has a lot to do with our innate coping and survival instincts. However, this tendency can prove to be counterproductive when it comes to your desire to leave the bitter pain of a troubled past in order to reach toward the promise of a bright future.

Because of how traumatizing the pain of the past can be, you often hear people say how difficult it is for them to forgive the offender who has seriously hurt them, whether physically or emotionally. This is evidence that we cannot so easily walk away from the hurts of our pasts without experiencing some intervening form of spiritual healing. And still there are many others who can truthfully admit that it is easier to forgive, but harder to forget.

The important point to keep in mind is that pain from the past is the chief culprit that prevents so many from moving forward. The saying "sticks and stones may break my bones, but words will never hurt me" is only true in the movies and TV shows. In real life, we find that words can indeed cause pain when used in an abusive manner.

...words can indeed cause pain when used in an abusive manner.

Unfortunately, many people commit suicide because of the unbearable pain that stems from unresolved childhood hurts. And along with suicide, you will also find marriages succumbing to divorce, people suffering from depression, and women turning to cosmetic surgery, all due in no small part to hurts endured in the past.

Stay Connected

You would be amazed at the number of people who alter their lives drastically all because of someone else's opinion. You may be one of those people. That is why it is imperative for you to stay connected to God. He is a reliable Source, and He causes you to connect with reliable people. Do not be mistaken! God will use man to fulfill His purposes in the earth.

You cannot discount the important role that others will play in helping you to achieve success in life. Just because many people have let you down, you must not make the mistake of trying to go at it alone. You just have to find the right people with whom to connect!

I FORGOT TO BE AFRAID

Someone may ask, "What should I look for in a person?" My answer is always, "look for qualities that are in line with the word of God!" Whether you are searching for a close friend, a trustworthy husband, a faithful wife, or a strong mentor, always refer to the word of God because the right connection determines whether you are successful or not.

But you must develop amnesia when it comes to your past relationships. Yes, man, she cheated on you! Yes, woman, she said that she would be a good friend in which to confide, but told your business to everybody! But you must make a choice to forget about those things. Your future is at stake! Your best is yet to come, if only you would determine to stay connected to the Source!

Your best is yet to come, only if you would determine to stay connected to the Source!

Over the years, I have heard people give too many excuses as to why things were not working out in their lives. Beloved, it starts with your connection. If you are connected to a bad tree, you are going to produce bad fruit! The branch can only produce its fruit from the nutrients found in the tree's roots system. So, if the tree is not planted in good soil, you cannot expect good fruit to be produced.

Therefore, stop using excuses! Uproot yourself from those bad relationships! Stop being afraid to take a leap of faith! Fear will tell you that it is okay to remain where you are because you may think, it can't get any better than this. But faith will tell you that it will be better when you disconnect. Refuse to settle, and choose to change!

Refuse to settle, and choose to change!

It is very dangerous to be connected to fear! Good fruit is never produced in such soil. It is like the fig tree that Jesus cursed because it did not produce figs at a time when they were supposed to come forth. Fear will paralyze you and cause you to think that everything is alright when things are not working out like they are supposed to. To put it plainly, whenever you are not operating in faith, it is a blatant slap in God face! He has provided the soil, the people, and the proper environment to help you to prosper, but you refuse to believe, instead choosing to settle for less than His best for you.

As Jesus suggested in Luke 13:7, whenever anything fails to produce as it should, it is wasting the nutrients from the soil. It might as well be extracted from the soil and burned! Likewise, whenever we fail to exude God's power and authority, we fail live up to our fullest potential. Beloved, please do not misunderstand me. I am not suggesting that anyone should commit suicide! I am only suggesting that you make the necessary changes in your life so that you can begin to produce the fruit that you were always designed to produce. I firmly believe that the world is yearning for us who live by faith to be exposed! We must be the ones who stand out and lead the way!

Choose to Forget!

You must make a conscience choice to develop amnesia when it comes to fear and failure. That is why your connection to God's way of doing things is very important. The right mentor will teach you how to train your mind to develop amnesia when it comes to operating in fear. The

Developing Amnesia

more failures you remember, the less effective you are. Therefore, connect to a mentor who will remind you of the great potential you possess.

I heard a well-known televangelist once say that fear is nourished by self-preservation. What a powerful truth!!! In other words, it is dangerous to think that you can stay on the path of faith without help. Anytime you depend on self, self will always remind you of the bad things that have happened in your life. However, when you open your life to people who have the ability to point you in the right direction, you will develop a pattern of success. That pattern in-turn will cause you to only remember how to operate by faith and how to forget to function by fear.

...fear is nourished by self-preservation.

CHAPTER 7

NO MORE EXCUSES!

7

NO MORE EXCUSES!

As is his custom, my mentor often shares many of his life stories with me and his other mentees. I am sure there are many reasons why, but the main reason, I believe, is that he wants us to avoid some of the same valleys and pitfalls that he went through earlier in his life. While there are some valleys that cannot be avoided, there are others that we should not try to steer clear of because of their benefit to our development.

I FORGOT TO BE AFRAID

Your faith is designed to keep you in the race for the long-haul.

These valleys are not designed to destroy us; they are our proving grounds! All faith must be tested for its authenticity. In other words, authentic faith will require that you go through and successfully pass certain trials to qualify your right to travel further along the path of your destiny. Your faith is designed to keep you in the race for the long-haul.

One of faith's many attributes is perseverance. My mentor often says that perseverance will always outlast persecution. When we walk by faith, there is no delay or denial!

Get Up and Do Something!

I recall one of those stories from my mentor that applies to this chapter. Earlier in his life, he was going through something rather significant in his life. People were ridiculing him, and I am sure he felt like the world was falling on top of him. But he has always made it a point to surround himself with people who would encourage him. He remembers one of those individuals saying to him, "Get up and stop giving those people something to talk about!" What a wake-up call! How many of us need to hear those same exact words? They may be bitter to your ears, but I guarantee that those words would be medicine to your soul!

As you should know from experience, nobody needs do encourage you to stay down when you are discouraged. During our darkest hours, we are often our worst critics. But you can also be your biggest fan! When there is no one else around to encourage you, you must learn to encourage yourself! And no matter what, you are always going to have naysayers. Some people are waiting for you to fail. In fact, they are banking on your failure.

God, the Fight Promoter?

You will rarely, if ever, hear pastors refer to God as a fight promoter. But my pastor had the audacity to refer to God as such! And I agree 100%! If you think about it, you would agree too. The fact that you are still alive and well is a testament to the

I FORGOT TO BE AFRAID

fact that God is a fight promoter...and a great one at that! Consider the many trials and battles you fought over the years. Understand that God arranged many of them Himself, all for your development. The others, sad to say, are the result of bad decision-making on our part.

The Bible tells us to fight the good fight of faith. For one, it is a good fight, which means it is a fixed fight! Your Promoter has ensured that all things will work out for your good because you love Him and are called according to His purpose! And secondly, never forget that it is an actual fight! That means you must be confrontational.

In my previous book "A Changed Perception", I talk extensively about the need for us to exercise tenacity when it comes to believing God to do something awesome in our lives. Things are not just going to fall into your lap. You must do something. But be assured that you will win...if you fight!

You must do something.

Early in his career, Mike Tyson dominated the sport of boxing. Many of his opponents could not last beyond the first round! His ability to totally overwhelm his opponents struck much fear into anyone who would dare challenge him. No one could even come close to beating him…until he came against someone who had nothing to lose!

The fight between Mike Tyson and James "Buster" Douglas was one for the record books! Buster's mother had passed away 23 days before the bout, so he definitely had something to fight for. Naturally, he was still mourning the loss of the one who delivered him into this world. When you lose someone close to you, you tend to look at life differently. Mike Tyson, on the other hand, was over-confident. He was at the top of his game and no opponent was ready for this type of boxer! Mike and his corner people were not prepared for what would happen next. Needless to say, Buster wound up winning the bout because he fought with purpose, to honor the memory of his mother.

Fight With a Strategy

If you realize that your fight has been fixed, or even if you had something to fight for, would you fight differently? Most people, particularly believers, do not believe their fight is fixed.

I FORGOT TO BE AFRAID

Therefore, the tendency is to enter into a fight without a successful strategy in mind. The only strategy that has ever succeeded in a God-fixed fight is one prescribed by the Fight Promoter Himself...the Word of God. Our first response to this strategy is to surrender to it. Again, the fight is fixed! It behooves us to surrender to a strategy that has been proven to work time and time again, throughout the ages.

Our first response to a strategy is to surrender to it.

The patriarch Daniel used this strategy and turned lions into pillows. His three friends implemented the same plan and survived a fiery furnace that was heated seven-times hotter than usual! King David surrendered to this plan and wound up fighting off a lion, a bear, and a 10-ft giant! Fast forward a few hundred years and you will see Jesus consistently putting this plan into action throughout His life. This plan works, but you must be willing to surrender to it and allow it to work in your life!

No More Excuses!

70

❦ FAITH STRATEGIES ❦
CHAPTER 1

WHO TOLD YOU TO BE AFRAID?

☞ And once you submit to fear, it will expose you for the coward you are.

☞ Faith is birthed in unity, while fear is birthed out of chaos.

☞ There are too many people in this world who simply do not know how to walk by faith.

☞ There's no need to worry when you operate in God's assurance.

CHAPTER 2

IT'S NOT THAT BIG A DEAL!

☞ Being "alone" is not always a bad position.

☞ Some things are simply not worth the time!

☞ The bark is designed to cloud your view of the truth.

☞ When life gets tough, you must choose to smile!

☞ You must get to the point where you are tired of striking out.

CHAPTER 3

WHAT ABOUT THE ECONOMY?

☞ Our heavenly nation tells us (citizens) that we are the head, and not the tail!

☞ God's economy will never fail!

☞ You cannot be fearful of giving.

☞ The Source is never absent of His resources.

CHAPTER 4

IT'S TIME FOR A NAME CHANGE

☞ God's word is always reliable!

☞ You now have direction in life because God's word is your compass.

☞ Faith demands corresponding action!

☞ I am the creator of my world!

☞ I am no longer a victim. I am a victor!!

CHAPTER 5

KICK THE HABIT

☞ Fear may be present, but faith always trumps fear!

☞ What matters is whether you are willing to fight the good fight of faith.

CHAPTER 6

DEVELOPING AMNESIA

☞ Words can indeed cause pain when used in an abusive manner.

☞ Your best is yet to come, if only you would determine to stay connected to the Source!

☞ Refuse to settle, and choose to change!

☞ Fear is nourished by self-preservation.

CHAPTER 7

NO MORE EXCUSES!

☞ Your faith is designed to keep you in the race for the long-haul.

☞ You must do something.

☞ Our first response to a strategy is to surrender to it.

NOTES

NOTES

NOTES

NOTES

ABOUT THE AUTHOR

S.D. Horton is a life coach, author, businessman, and religious leader who resides in New Mexico with his family. He is an ordained minister with nearly 20 years of experience in counseling and other ministry work. Without compromising the integrity of his message, Horton is extremely gifted in his ability to utilize poignant, anecdotal humor to entertain and educate his audiences, keeping him in constant demand as an inspirational speaker.

Attain a better life!!

Testimonial:
- This book has enabled me to realize that my gifts and talents need to be shared with the world. Horton's quote 'a gift not shared is a gift not worth having' has caused me to experience success as an accomplished restaurateur and established businessman.
                              - Restaurant Manager

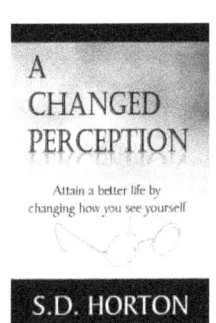

A Changed Perception

This book will show you how to:
 - Change the way you see yourself
 - Know that you were born to succeed
 - Do the opposite of what you've been doing that led you to failure
 - Do the right things in order to consistently get the right results
 - And much more...

Order your copy today from my website, www.sdhorton.com

Living Waters Series!!!

A FLOW OF ENCOURAGEMENT FOR
The Married Couple

Exposing the secrets of maintaining a healthy marriage

$9.95

Living Waters: A Flow of Encouragement For the Married Couple

In reading this book, you will be able to::
- Learn key points in how to effectively communicate with your spouse
- Understand the difference between love and purpose
- Realize how the two of you can successfully become one
- And much more...

Order from www.lulu.com

SD Horton Enterprises

Message from the CEO:

SD Horton Enterprises is here to provide quality assistance for your inspirational and writing needs. We currently offer the following services:

- Speaking Engagements
- Conference/Seminar Hosting
- Life Coaching Sessions
- Proofreading / Editorial Services

To book S.D. Horton as a guest speaker at your event, email your request to horton@sdhorton.com For more information, visit our website at www.sdhorton.com.

-S.D. Horton

www.ingramcontent.com/pod-product-compliance
Lightning Source LLC
Chambersburg PA
CBHW020015050426
42450CB00005B/479